What To Look For?
~ A Full Guide On Reading The Strata Documents ~

First Edition

Wilson Lam, REALTOR®, SRES®, ABR®

Copyright © 2018 Wilson Lam

All rights reserved.

ISBN: 9781791829162

For my dad, David Lam –

Throughout my whole life, all I wanted to do is to be someone who you can be proud of and consider as successful. But I failed to meet your standard, failed many many times... to a point that I feel shameful and tired. All I have left is tears in my eyes... Because I'm already a grown man, you are an old man, and I have done nothing for you. I don't know how this book will turn out for me, but I hope it can be a turning point in where I can stop letting you down. Then I can spend more time with you, share more memories together.
I love you Dad.

CONTENTS

	Acknowledgments	i
1	What's included in the Strata Documents	1
2	Form B	4
3	Financial Statement	11
4	Strata Plan	12
5	Depreciation Report	14
6	Engineering Report	17
7	Strata Minutes	19
8	Insurance	26
9	Bylaws & Rules	28
10	Other Important Documents	30
11	Conclusion	33

ACKNOWLEDGMENTS

A Special thanks to my managing broker at Regent Park Realty Inc., Mr. Xen Taam for helping me in all these years to become a knowledgeable and professional real estate agent.

A big thank you to all my past clients who gave me the opportunities to serve them, for trusting me, and for widening my knowledge through the buying process on different strata units.

Thank you to my dearest wife, Seena Zhang, for loving me and supporting me all the time; especially those little nudges to keep me moving forward and improving in life.

Thank you Lord God for saving my life, and to show me what unconditional love is. I am thankful for all the angels you placed beside me, so I can keep going.

1

WHAT'S INCLUDED IN THE STRATA DOCUMENTS?

When we look at Strata Documents, we want to know the history of the building; if the building is well managed? If it is financially healthy? Will there be big ticket items that need to be paid right away? paid soon? In other words, checking the strata documents is a safety check for risks and liabilities you will be taking on as a buyer if move forward in purchasing the property.

While reviewing all the strata documents, highlight the things you don't understand and ask your Realtor. Your Realtor, who also known as the Buyer's agent is your resources on providing answers to all your questions in regards to the real estate transaction. In British Columbia, if you choose the listing agent to write you the offer, you are the unrepresented party and the listing agent has no obligation to explain to you in anything. Also, it is the Buyer's responsibility to check if everything provided is legit and up to your standard. Once you buy the property and find out something is wrong, you do have the right to sue the seller and their agent, but you will have no ground against them if you did not do your due diligence before buying or you will have a hard time proving to the judge that the information provided was intentionally trick you into a trap of buying the property.

Therefore, it is very important to check everything thoroughly or have someone professional whom you can trust to do the checking for you. Let's say if you do not have an agent and you have questions in regards to the building while reading the strata documents, who can you ask? You may gather all your questions and left a voicemail for the Strata Manager to call you back because this person would be a professional who is non-bias from buying or selling the property. However, the Strata Manager / Strata Agent may not call you back, because they have no obligation to share information with someone who is not a resident/owner of the strata. Most of the time strata agent is friendly and they will call you back, but they are busy people who manage multiple buildings so it may take them a few days to reply call(s) / email(s). Please start early in reviewing your strata documents so you will have enough time before the subject removal date to decide whether this unit is the right fit

What To Look For?
~ A Full Guide On Reading The Strata Documents ~

for you. In a nutshell, for the amount that you are paying to purchase this property, are you willing to accept the risk that this building carries?

2

FORM B

The Strata Form B is a document that the strata management company sells to the Seller or their agent (Realtor / Lawyer) when selling a home. It is an information certificate signed by the strata manager confirming that all the information provided are correct and are best of the strata manager's knowledge of the building, which these are information from the management company's record provided by the developer, previous management company(-ies), and the most updated information based on the result of the most recent Annual General Meeting (AGM). The Strata Form B will come with the following information: the current strata fee of this unit, if there is any money owing by this unit to the strata, are there any special levy(-ies) and for how much, any lawsuit against the strata, how much is the current contingency fund (savings), how many parking stalls and/or

What To Look For?
~ A Full Guide On Reading The Strata Documents ~

storage locker included with this unit, if there were any renovation approval), how many unit(s) is/are currently rented (called the Form J), etc.

Strata Fee:

Understand what is included in the strata fee. Some buildings have strata fees that include your utilities, different facilities, maybe a 24-hour concierge, some may even include your property tax, etc. If strata fee is relatively high, is worth looking into it to find out why. It does not automatically mean that the building is mismanaged. Did the building recently clear out their savings for repair and maintenance which now they are rebuilding their contingency fund? Or maybe after reviewing the depreciation report the strata learned that there will be a few large ticket items to be paid out in the next few years so they are saving up for those potential expenses? Is the building trying to avoid having a special levy, so their management style is to keep a higher strata fee? Or the building was just simply mismanaged? With a relatively low strata fee, could it be that the building hired a very handy caretaker who could fix most of the issues? Maybe they have saved a good amount of contingency fund that they can be relaxed on the strata fee? Or maybe the strata have minimal facilities or next to no facility features which allow them to have fewer expenses? Or the building is self-managed so they could save some money from paying to a management company? Or simply the strata charges a special levy every year to each unit to maintain a low strata fee? Whatever the reason, you will have to find out and see if it is reasonable for you.

Money owing:

There are many reasons why there is money owing to the strata, maybe the owner lost a job, has family issues, accumulated fines from violating the bylaws, charged late fees, penalties, special levy charges, etc. However, your lawyer will look at this and make sure that the Seller's lawyer will pay off these monies before the unit get transferred to you. Reviewing this portion gives you a chance to learn the background of the Seller and what type of person you are dealing with, more than to identify any risk you should be aware of.

Special Levy owing:

In a lot of the older buildings, this is why the Seller has to sell because they cannot afford to pay off the special levy. This could be thousands of dollars and again your lawyer will look after this for you.

Lawsuits against the strata:

If you see this, this is something worth calling the Strata Agent about. The Form B will include extra pages about which unit in the building is suing the strata and for what reason. You should

What To Look For?
~ A Full Guide On Reading The Strata Documents ~

find out how long has the lawsuit been and at what stage is it right now. The Strata Agent will let you know in his/her educated guess if this is something that should resolve soon or it will be dragged on for a longer time. A red flag would be if a good number of units gathered to sue the strata for mismanaging the building or something more serious like discrimination.

Contingency fund:

This is the money reserved for the building's repair and maintenance. A formula that Realtors use is to take the contingency fund and divide it by the total number of strata unit in the building. The answer to this formula gives us a rough estimation of how much money does each strata unit have for savings. If the number comes out to be $1,000 or less, that means the strata does not have enough money save up and they may need to charge special levy or the strata fee will increase in the next AGM (the percentage of increase will be determined at the AGM). If the amount is between $1,001 to $2,999, the strata are on track. If the amount is $3,000 or above, this is a healthy strata corporation and you should not have to worry about this building being the poor strata that always asking for money. Does that mean if the strata have less than $1,000 per strata unit in the contingency fund, it is considered as a red flag? Not always, you also have to study the strata to see if they just recently finished paying out the money to some big-ticket items like roof replacement, elevator replacement, building envelope replacement, fixing a major water leak, re-piping to all the drains, etc. If they did pay out a few major renovations or repairments which there are no other pricy items lining up for the next few years, you should still be safe.

Parking & Locker:

In most newer buildings, the developer set the parking and locker as limited common properties, meaning that you will have the exclusive use of the parking and locker but the area is being managed by the strata and regulated under the strata bylaws. In some older buildings, you may see parking and locker as separate strata lot with a separate land title; then you will have to make sure that your lawyer also transfers you those separate title(s). Or in some other buildings, your parking and locker are just common properties. It really depends on how the developer set them up in the very beginning, but the same setup remains despite the number of times the unit get sold and get transferred. What problem that may arise is the number of parking stall and/or locker shown on the listing does not match with the Strata Form B. This trouble may happen if the 1st hand buyer bought extra parking stall(s) from the developer, has been occupying on the extra parking stall(s) for years but the proper paperwork was never given to the management company to keep on file. In this case, ask the Seller and/or the listing agent to provide the

What To Look For?
~ A Full Guide On Reading The Strata Documents ~

proof for the strata management company to update the Form B. If the Seller cannot provide this proof, even though the Seller has been occupying more parking stall(s), after you have purchased this unit, you may only have the right to use the stall(s) provided with the unit as per documentation. Strata Management company needs paper proof or paper trail to go by for this type of record change. This applies also with purchasing a 2nd hand new development unit and a 2nd presale unit. If you are losing a parking stall or a storage locker, your purchase price should reflect that, so look carefully.

Renovation Approval:

The Seller may have claimed that they have done some upgrades to the unit, but all renovations must be approved by the strata council or the owner may get fines for violating the bylaws. Also, the strata may have a standard requirement that the owner has to follow in order to get the approval; for example, the laminate floor has to have a minimum thickness and the underlay must meet a certain requirement for soundproof. These approval documents would be included in the Strata Form B. Note that if the unit got approval from the Strata for renovation, it does not mean they got a city permit. Anytime a renovation involving plumbing and gas connection must require a city permit. Electrical may or may not require a city permit which depends on the situation.

Units being rented:

This list is important if the building has a rental restriction for a certain percentage of the building. If it is at its max, that means you will have to be on the waiting list in order to get your unit rented out. The wait varies and it could be as long as a few years.

3

FINANCIAL STATEMENT

The key in looking at these documents is to see if the strata run positively in their cash flow. Do they always go over budget? It is mainly to see whether the strata management knows what they are doing. The biggest item in a strata's expenses is the insurance premium. If you have a background in accounting, you may understand more on how to process these documents/numbers. If not, ask a friend who can help. Someone who has more background in strata expenses would be able to tell if the numbers on the financial statement are reasonable.

4

STRATA PLAN

The Strata Plan is an official document with measurements on the area of the building and is registered in land title office. Real estate agent uses it as a reference to the square footage of the unit when listing the property. However, it may not be the actual measurement because the strata plan is not an as-built drawing. Therefore, some Realtors would hire a third-party measuring company to measure the unit and come up with larger square footage, but a conservative buyer's agent would still use the strata plan because it is an official document that is registered with the land title office. We also use the strata plan with the land title to see if the strata lot number shown on the land title match the unit on the strata plan. Rarely there would be differences but is good to double check. Also, the strata plan would show if your parking stall was set up with a strata lot number, if it was a limited common property or if it was a common property that the individual stalls would not be shown on the strata plan.

On the strata plan, you may find a chart with one or two columns, one says Unit Entitlement and other says Interest Upon Destruction. Unit entitlement is used to calculate your strata fee and special levies, it is your portion of the entire building that you have to chip in. Interest upon destruction is used by the insurance company if the building was destroyed and they would use this chart to pay out the owners. Another scenario is that the building was bought out by a developer and the developer would also use this chart to pay out the owners. Both unit entitlement and interest upon destruction were being calculated differently by professional surveyors/engineers and would be used in different ways; however, the rule changed and strata plans filed after July 1st, 2000 will not have the schedule of interest upon destruction.

5

DEPRECIATION REPORT

A Depreciation Report is a thick document done by an engineering firm or an architectural company who would dissect the building for an estimated lifespan of every component of the building. The second part of the report gives a minimum 3 timelines on how the building can prepare the funding to pay for the repairs or replacements. One timeline is to increase the strata fee enough that the strata would not require a special levy to pay off these costs. The other extreme is to keep strata fee low and ask owners for special levy every time when repair and replacement costs appear. The last timeline would show the middle of the two methods where the strata fee will be adjusted enough to save for contingency funds and when the years with large item expenses arrived, the strata would ask for a special levy. It is important to find out which method the strata have adopted

What To Look For?
~ A Full Guide On Reading The Strata Documents ~

and if you can agree to how the strata are being managed. Note that the lifespans on the report for each of the component are only an estimation, so they may last longer without problem or may break down earlier than what had written on the report. The only way to find out which method the strata adopted or none of the method, you would have to read the minutes carefully and to check out the budget plan if the numbers match the one on depreciation report.

Since 2013, the BC government made it mandatory for all strata with more than four lots to have a depreciation report; however, strata corporations would still have the option to vote it off on the strata's Annual General Meeting. The benefit of having this report is for the strata corporation to plan for the future and to save enough money for all these future costs. Before the law has passed, there were strata corporations that did not plan ahead and had insufficient contingency funds to pay for all the breakdowns of the building, so the strata had to impose a large special levy on the owners, where some owners could not afford the levy and were forced to be foreclosed.

Since there are so many benefits of having a depreciation report, why would some strata still vote it off? It is because the cost of producing this report is around $30 to $50 thousand dollars which the strata are not planning on paying, or some old strata may have planned to sell the whole complex off to a developer within a few years. The report must be updated every three years unless voted it off in an AGM / SGM, but there is another cost associated with getting the updated report.

To use this document to our benefit, we look at what are the big-ticket items coming up in the next few years. Most major big-ticket items are roof replacement, elevator replacement, building envelope replacement (sidings, balconies), re-piping (changing the water pipes & drainage pipes), etc. Other mid-ticket items would be window replacement, replacing the HVAC (air) system, replacing the hot water tank, upgrading the security system, etc. The report would have a dollar figure beside each item, so even though each building is not the same, you are able to understand what costs that may potentially appear in the next few years. We would cross-reference with the strata minutes to see what has been replaced, paid out and what has been deferred.

6

ENGINEERING REPORT

All strata building comes with a 2-5-10 warranty provided by the developer. The warranty covers all various structural, mechanical and cosmetic components till 2 years it was built. Building envelope will be covered till 5 years. The structure of the building will be covered for up to 10 years. When the warranty is near expired, the strata council would hire an engineering company to assess the building for any deficiencies that might be addressed by the warranty. Using the report, the strata may get the developer to come back and fix all the deficiencies. Sometimes the report addresses some problems but the developer is not willing to fix these deficiencies. When this problem arises, strata will claim the warranty so the warranty company will be the middle person in dealing with this issue. Worst comes to worst, the strata would have to pay for fixing all deficiencies first and claim insurance on it. By reading the report, you will know if this building is well built and if this developer a good developer. Always cross-reference with the minutes to know what's going on in the building.

7

STRATA MINUTES

There are 3 different types of minutes: Strata Council Meeting Minutes (CM), Annual General Meeting Minutes (AGM), and Special General Meeting Minutes (SGM). Every year at the AGM, the new Strata Council is being formed through votes from all owners. All owners would also have a chance to vote for decisions on any big issues like special levy and changes that are proposed for the bylaws; once they reach quorum or ¾ votes, the changes or decisions will be adopted. The bylaws with the new changes will be registered at the land title office. Therefore, it is very important to read the AGM first and to see what are the new changes and big decisions happening with the building. After finished reading the AGM, read the SGM. Special General Meetings are not mandatory. It only happens when it is not yet time for the AGM to be held but a major decision has to be made right away. Issues that may arise at the SGM are the change of strata management company, major renovations, the charge of a special levy, etc.

Last but not least is your CM minutes. Your Realtor usually would ask for the last 2 years of minutes from the listing agent. Rarely in a special request, you may ask for 3 years of minutes but that means the listing agent would have to get that from the Seller or order it from the Strata Management Company. That takes time, money and effort, so the listing agent who has the right to refuse would probably refuse. You will need a very good reason why you want all 3 years of minutes or even more. Maybe you have heard a rumor that something bad happened in the building further than 2 years and you must verify that before buying. However, prepare yourself that you may not get this information so would you still buy it?

What is the standard frequency of having a strata council meeting? There is no set rule, it is up to your council members to decide how often the meeting should be held. Not every strata council likes to have a meeting every month, they may decide to meet every other month, every quarterly, every half a year, or even once a year. To know when is the next council meeting or if there's a missing meeting minutes, read the last line of the minutes. At the end of every minutes, they might schedule for the next meeting. Although they may change

What To Look For?
~ A Full Guide On Reading The Strata Documents ~

the date afterward, you would still have a rough idea when the next meeting would be and be able to predict whether you are missing a minutes or not. Is better to read the most recent minutes and reading them backward in time. The reason for that is because the most recent minutes is the most relevant and the issues in the oldest minutes may have been solved or no longer issues.

What are the issues that you should be aware of? Security is one of the biggest concerns. You want to stay in a safe place. If units, cars, mailboxes, lockers kept being broken into, maybe it is not a good neighbourhood. How did the strata improve their security? Did the break-in continue? Sometimes hallway furniture and paintings get stolen, the minutes should have all these recorded. The strata could spend money on installing security cameras, increase the number of surveillance cameras, hire security pratol, install a gate or box-off the mailboxes, but still not be effective on keeping the thieves away. More people are moving into metro Vancouver which creates a ripple effect where there is a growing disparity between the rich and the poor. More thieves are in the city, break-ins are becoming more common. The question for you as the buyer to think about is, does the frequency of security break-ins acceptable? Are you satisfied with how the strata handle the issue? From reading the minutes, do you have an impression that the strata management has security issues under control?

Floods or water damages inside the building may cost a lot of financial burden to a strata building. This could be the result of the building being old, being poorly built, having a design flaw, or it could be man-made negligence. If the building still has a 2-5-10 new home warranty, fixing costs may still be recovered by the developer or the warranty, but if the building is old the strata have to come up with the money on fixing such issue when it arises. The biggest problem in water damage is from man-made negligence, where the building has to first claim insurance and the building insurance company investigate the cause of the water damage and charge back to the owner for their negligence and they would claim into their own insurance. Man-made negligence could be a resident's washer broke or the toilet broke where it flooded the entire floor and the few floors below, a resident who wanted to have a bath and forgot to turn off the tap on the bathtub, or resident decided to hang their laundry onto a water sprinkler. The insurance company will move the affected residences into the hotel and hire a restoration company to fix all affected areas including the homes of the affected residences. The repairment process could take months to complete and the bill is huge! Other water leaks could be from an old roof that needs to be fixed or replaced or the old water pipes that burst and need to be replaced or re-piped. The strata may have fixed these issues using the

What To Look For?
~ A Full Guide On Reading The Strata Documents ~

strata's money or claim through the building insurance company. If many claims went through the building insurance in a short period of time, the insurance company may not renew the insurance policy, or the insurance premium may significantly increase when renewing their policy.

Another issue you may find in strata minutes would be the problem where too many residents cannot afford to pay their strata fees or not paying them on time. The building needs money to run, including the management company's fee, caretaker's salary, utilities, repair and maintenance, insurance premium, garbage disposal, gardening, snow plowing, lightbulb changing, etc. If people cannot afford to pay for their strata fee and special levy, then it is a problem. The strata corporation may have applied for a court order on the unit and forced the unit to foreclose in order to recover the strata fee, special levy, late fee, and interest. More often you see many units are for sale in an old building because the proposed large special levy has passed in a recent AGM or SGM and many owners cannot afford to pay it off. In a slow housing market, if these units cannot be sold, they may end up in a foreclosure situation.

Politics could also be a big issue when you see all strata council members get voted off in an AGM, there could have been a conflict within the residents on how the building should be managed. Lawsuit may suck dry the strata's contingency fund. That does not mean you should not buy into a building if there is a lawsuit but depends on what the lawsuit is about and on which stage the process is on, you may want to avoid into buying a unit in those buildings.

How to find out more? Usually, buyers rely on their Realtor to investigate and get a better understanding of the situation, that means talking to the listing agent and calling the Strata Manager. However, this gets tricky because listing agent's words are not reliable and Strata Manager has no obligation to answer questions from people outside of the strata. What does that mean? In court, the buyer must do their due diligence before purchasing the property. If you bring the seller and their parties to court claiming that you did not know about this issue and you blame the seller for not providing you this information, you may lose the case because buyer must do their own due diligence. If you claim in court that the information provided is fake, where the seller knew there was a problem and they were trying to cover it, it is a different scenario and you would have to prove to the judge how you come up with this conclusion. That's why it is very important to check with the city on the history of the property, the strata management company on things you do not understand in the strata documents, and even newspaper if something happened before that was reported on the news. About the Strata Manager, the strata

What To Look For?
~ A Full Guide On Reading The Strata Documents ~

manager is hired by the strata to manage the building, so they are hired by the strata and serve the people inside the strata. You as the purchaser and your agent do not belong in the strata so strata managers have the right to ignore phone calls and emails from people outside the strata. When they return your phone calls and emails, it is based on goodwill. You may not like this but this is the fact you should understand. By reading the strata minutes, you learn a lot about the building, the background, the people and the management style. If risks are tolerable you will purchase the property; if not, do not buy and move to the next!

8

INSURANCE

As mentioned in earlier chapters, insurance is the biggest expense in a building. It usually takes up 1/3 of the building expenses. Like any other insurance policy, the premium is calculated based on the amount of risk the insurance company has to take. When there are "too many" claims, the insurance company has the right not renewing the policy at the renewal date or renewing the policy at a significantly large increase on the premium. What's being "too many" is determined by the insurance company, which could be more than one claim per year or more than one claim in a consecutive year. The highest I have seen in a deductible was $200,000. The risk of having a high deductible is that if anything happened to the building that caused by your unit, the strata will ask you to pay the deductible and you better have insurance that will cover that deductible amount. When you buy your insurance policy, make sure the premium you pay will cover the building's deductible or you will be the person paying the difference of what your insurance is willing to pay out and the amount you have to pay back to the building's insurance company.

9

BYLAWS & RULES

Every strata corporation starts with the generic set of bylaws called the standard bylaws. To change the bylaws, the strata has to reach quorum or ¾ of the votes in order to pass and take effect. This will happen only in AGM/SGM. If the strata changed wordings or added new laws like the rental restriction or pet restriction to the bylaws, the effective date will be written on a separate page attached to the front of the bylaw when it was registered through the land title office. On the other hand, rules can be changed freely by the strata council during the strata council meeting. For new buildings, amenities like gym room, party room, swimming pool, hot tub, barbecue area, music room, study room, yoga room, basketball court, badminton court, theatre room, etc... cannot be used before the rules are written by the strata management and approved by the strata council. Some strata

What To Look For?
~ A Full Guide On Reading The Strata Documents ~

may have very rigid rules and fines on visitor parking, move-in/move-out, and garbage room. Please make sure you pay attention to these items and see if they are acceptable for you. Sometimes strata councils are so harsh on the residences, it created a lot of tensions which can turn into politics. It is a good idea to cross reference with the minutes and learn about the strata.

10

OTHER IMPORTANT DOCUMENTS

Land Title is important because you need to know if the person selling the property to you is the same person on the title. Check the name on the title and make sure the name matches what it is written on the offer. Same with the property descriptions. It is also important to know if there are restrictive covenants, liens, easements, right of way on the title that may affect you. What are these things? Restrictive covenants are restrictions added onto the land usually by the developer before it gets sold to you. It is usually about the building scheme, the outlook of the property, but true enough when you see a restriction on your property, it would be wise to find out what is being restricted and why it is being restricted. A Lien is a charge or owing on your property. For strata units, you

What To Look For?
~ A Full Guide On Reading The Strata Documents ~

may see the strata corporation had placed a lien on the unit claiming for the owing money. Meaning that if the property gets sold, the strata may get the money back from the sales. Your lawyer or notary public who is responsible for this transaction will sort that all out and make sure it is a clear title before it gets transferred under your name. The easements and the right of way to grant the easement/right of way holder to have access onto your property. Usually, it would be the electric company to fix the power line, the municipality to fix the water/sewer, the cabling company to do your phone line, internet and tv cable etc. If the easement/right of way holder is not one of the service providers nor the municipality, then you better find out who it is. For single family homes, you would have to be more careful but for strata units, it is common that a big building has many pipes and wires underneath the ground. Your municipality would have an interactive map that shows what is on or underneath your property.

A Property Disclosure Statement is a survey filled by the Seller on the best of his/her knowledge about this property. It has 4 pages and the Seller would have to sign it to make it effective. As the Buyer, you would read through the yes or no questionnaire and see if there are anything abnormal. What's abnormal should be provided with more information on the comment section. If there is no explanation, or if there is any missing signature, please ask the

Seller to complete the PDS before you sign back and accept this form.

The PDS and the Land Title if not specified are not part of the contract. Therefore, please mention on the contract that the land title and the PDS form part of the contract so the Seller is responsible for providing the truth for this information and make them reliable if something wrong happens.

11

CONCLUSION

At the end of the day, it is your responsibility to read and understand all the strata documents before accepting them and removing your subjects. Please be aware that although your Realtor should have helped you in reviewing the documents and identify the potential risks, they are not fully reliable for reading your documents. Plus, your Realtor is not you! He/she would never be able to fully understand your standard on what you can accept and not accept in the strata documents. Therefore, I write this book and hope that you can expand your knowledge, to be less stressful, and be more joyful throughout the process. After reviewing all the strata documents, ask yourself this question: "for the price that I am paying for this property, am I willing to accept the risks and responsibilities involved with this building?" Price is a relative factor. You always need data to support your decision, and to determine if you are paying too much, buying at the right price, or would be paying too much. However, it also depends if you are in a hot market or a slow market. In a hot market, paying too much today could mean purchasing into a good deal for tomorrow, so it all depends. Or if you find your perfect dream home, you might be willing to pay more! Once you have found the very beloved home, you may be willing to accept more risks that come with the building. Yet buying a property involved a lot in your personal preferences and emotional factors. Whenever you find yourself not clear, always ask until you get a clear answer. If you are still confused, you have the full right not to proceed with the deal before you sign the paperwork. Is better if you give up early than to enter into a potential risk. Purchasing a property is an exciting life moment, but it could be very stressful too. I wish you all the best in finding your new home and have a very smooth transition! God bless you!

www.ingramcontent.com/pod-product-compliance
Lightning Source LLC
Chambersburg PA
CBHW072033230526
45468CB00021B/1684